FREE BOOKS

GET UNLIMITED FREE KINDLE BOOKS FROM OVERDRIVE, YOUR PUBLIC LIBRARY, AMAZON'S KINDLE LENDING LIBRARY, AND OTHER FREE SOURCES

By Steve Weber

Published by Stephen W. Weber
978-1-936560-27-1

Contents

Get Free Books from the Kindle Owner's Lending Library

Free books. Does anything on earth rival free reads? Perhaps free beer. Maybe free pizza. But that's it, as far as I'm concerned.

It's been a slippery slope. Way back in 2005, Amazon.com announced a new program called "Prime." It was a simple proposition: pay $79 a year for the annual membership, and you'd get free two-day shipping on most of my orders. Plus, you could upgrade to overnight shipping at a huge discount—just a few dollars per order.

I'm plenty thrifty, but Amazon didn't need to twist my arm before I coughed up my $79 fee for a Prime membership. It was a no-brainer. I order something from Amazon at least once or twice a week—books, groceries, electronic gadgets (the list has grown every year). So I didn't need to scribble the numbers on the back of an envelope to see that my annual Prime membership would pay for itself within a few months. Easily!

In the decade since then, Amazon has increased the Prime membership fee just $20. Meanwhile, the company has stacked up more and more benefits to Prime, much beyond the special shipping deals that attracted me at the start:

- Free monthly rentals of popular Kindle ebooks, thanks to the Kindle Owners' Lending Library. Anyone with a Kindle device and a Prime membership qualifies for the freebies, up to one book per month, with no due date.
- A personalized streaming music service that might render CDs and radios obsolete.
- Free on-demand streaming of movies and TV shows. The service, called Amazon Instant Video, is similar to Netflix's online video service. And while Amazon's video store doesn't yet match Netflix's selection, Amazon is gaining rapidly.

Whether you're like me—someone for whom Amazon Prime is a must-have—or a more infrequent Amazon customer—this book will explain how to get the most bang out of your Prime bucks.

Since you're reading this book, you probably have several questions about Prime—what it is, and how to use it best. Let's get started:

Borrowing from the Lending Library using an E-Ink or Paperwhite Kindle:

1. On the home screen, click on the shopping cart to visit the Kindle Store.
2. On the top navigation bar, click the menu button on the right edge.
3. From the pop-up menu, click **Kindle Owners' Lending Library**.
4. Browse the books eligible for borrowing.
5. Select a book to reveals its description page. Click **Borrow for Free**.

How many books may I borrow and for how long?

You may borrow one book at a time, with no due dates. You can borrow a new book as frequently as once a month, and you'll be prompted to return the book you're already borrowing.

If I finished a book before the month is over, can I borrow another book?

If you've already borrowed a book in the current calendar month, you must wait until the next calendar month to borrow another book. Unused borrowing eligibility doesn't roll over into subsequent months.

Get Kindle Freebies and Discounts from Websites

One of the best things about Amazon's digital bookstore is that many of its most popular books are offered completely free of charge during brief promotional periods. If you manage to find and download a book while it's offered free, it's yours to keep—forever. It's a great way to sample a new genre, or perhaps discover an author you hadn't noticed before.

This section of the book will describe a series of websites designed to help you locate free Kindle books. The first, KindleBuffet.com, is dear to my heart: I'm the founding publisher and update the site each day.

Yes, I love downloading free books to my Kindles so much, I started the website and newsletter called KindleBuffet.com to help keep track of the very best books currently available free. (The free promotions usually last only a few days, but there's a new crop every day). Take a look, and I'm sure you'll be amazed at the wealth of great books—usually there are several hundred freebies in virtually every category of fiction and nonfiction, every day of the year. And these aren't just the dogs that nobody wants, the selection includes bona-fide bestsellers from the most famous authors in the world. You may never have to pay for a book again! Heaven knows I've already downloaded more books than I'd be able to read in three lifetimes. But there's two things I've never been able to refuse—free food and free books.

Of the thousands of new books made available every day, I whittle the list down to highlight only the best on Kindle Buffet . For this, I use a two simple yardsticks: how many five-star reviews have Amazon customers posted about the book? Then, to skim the cream a bit more, I compare a book's number of positive reviews versus negative reviews. Although individual reviewers frequently disagree about a given book—and Amazon certainly has its share of knuckleheads offering their two-cents' worth—the bottom line is usually clear: the best, most widely enjoyed books attract the most (and best percentage of) positive reviews.

Kindle Buffet also has bestseller lists, updated hourly, of free Kindle books for every Amazon category—fiction, romance, business, cookbooks—you name it. So if you'd like to load up your Kindle with plenty of great reading material without spending a dime, visit www.KindleBuffet.com.

If you're curious as to why authors and publishers sometimes offer their books free in Kindle format, the answer is pretty simple: it boosts overall sales, especially for authors who've written a series of books. Sure, a few sales are "lost" for a certain title while it's free, but the word-of-mouth generated by the Kindle giveaway usually boosts sales of the author's other titles.

No Kindle? No problem!

Recently Amazon's line of Kindle devices have gotten so inexpensive it's hard to resist buying at least one. But you don't need any of Amazon's hardware to enjoy Kindle books. Amazon offers free Kindle apps for nearly every brand of cellphone, tablet, and desktop computer. For that matter, you can read Kindle books in a Web browser.

One footnote: In a coming section, we'll discuss how to "borrow" Kindle books, and for that you'd need a Kindle device.

More sites for finding Kindle freebies

As I mentioned, I have a special interest in Kindle Buffet since it's my baby. But there are several worthy competitors, and I'll list them here. Each has a different focus that you might find useful. Kindle Buffet's main attraction is that its "Editor's Picks" section focuses on the very best Kindle books currently offered free, so if your reading time is limited, Kindle Buffet might be an effective time-saver. Some of the other sites, however, offer a more complete selection. Also, some of the other sites accept advertising from authors who pay to have their books featured. Nothing wrong with that, except that it results in these sites recommending some truly awful books from time to time.

Like Kindle Buffet, the sites mentioned here participate in the Amazon Services LLC Associates Program, an affiliate program that pays advertising fees for linking to Amazon.com. While this list isn't exhaustive, these sites are among the best:

Pixelofink.com

Pixel of Ink offers a daily selection of free Kindle books and hot deals, which includes bargain Kindle books priced under $1, under $3, or under $5. If you're a reader of Christian or Faith-based literature, you'll want to check out this site's "Inspired Reads" section.

ereadernewstoday.com

Ereader News Today features free Kindle books, Kindle accessories, bargain Kindle books, and "book of the day" selections.

fkbooksandtips.com

Free Kindle Books and Tips publishes Kindle Daily Deals, daily selections of free Kindle books and apps. This site also includes helpful tutorials and shortcuts for using your Kindle.

kindlenationdaily.com

Kindle Nation Daily publishes Kindle picks, tips, news and commentary, and includes sections on Kindle apps and children's books. You can search for all currently available free Kindle books here.

http://www.ereaderiq.com

eReaderIQ has extensive listings of freebies and temporarily discounted Kindle books. You can also set up watch lists, so you'll know as soon as books by your favorite authors become free or discounted.

Borrow Books From your Public Library

The advent of eBooks was supposed to put the old-fashioned public library out of business, according to many pundits. But somebody forgot to tell the libraries this, and meanwhile they've been building collections for their customers who enjoy Kindle books and other digital content.

OverDrive (www.overdrive.com) an eBook service affiliated with thousands of local public libraries, enabling them to loan Kindle books and audiobooks. That's right, at most libraries nowadays you can borrow Kindle books at no charge, without even leaving the house. The best part: the collection of Kindle books available at most libraries includes bestsellers and classics from your favorite authors—precisely those books missing from KU.

Signing up for OverDrive is easy: First, download the app or go to their website and enter your library branch and card number. It's a service you're subsidizing with your tax dollars, so there's no reason not to try it.

Here's a variation of the experiment we discussed earlier: Go through a list of the books you've purchased over the past year. How many of them are available as a free Kindle loan from your library? More than you might expect.

The selection of Kindle books varies from library to library. Libraries in high-population areas tend to have a better selection, but many rural libraries have a nice collection too. And you're not necessarily limited to local library branches—in most states you can obtain a library card outside your immediate area at no extra charge. Also, several urban libraries will issue cards to out-of-state residents, although sometimes an annual fee is charged. For example, the Brooklyn Public Library, in New York, has an excellent selection of Kindle books and issues cards through the mail to any U.S. resident who pays an annual $50 fee. For a list of such libraries, consult this page: bit.ly/ebookLoans .

If you've tried checking out eBooks from the library in the past and have been disappointed, you should try again. Libraries have beefed up their digital selection tremendously in the past few years. Who knows, after you exhaust the available Kindle books at your local library, you might not have any time left to peruse KU.

I recently checked to see which of the top 10 books on the *New York Times* bestseller list were available through KU. Not a single one. But all 10 of those bestsellers were available as a Kindle loan through my local library. And of those 10 books, nine were also available as an audiobook download from my library. Buying those audiobooks from Amazon would have cost $218.55, whether I had a KU subscription or not.

But perhaps you don't read bestsellers; perhaps you prefer a steady diet of something more specific—like military science-fiction pulp novels. Maybe you're into kinky erotica. In that case you'll likely find a steady diet of such fare on KU alone.

In some ways your library's OverDrive service and KU are complementary. OverDrive tends to provide access to popular, mainstream books that librarians know will be in demand with a high percentage of their patrons. Meanwhile, KU includes books that simply aren't available to libraries—including quirky, innovative books from up-and-coming authors.

Although you don't need to physically visit the library to borrow Kindle books via OverDrive, you might have to wait in a virtual line for popular books. Libraries have a limited number of licenses for each eBook, so if all the available copies are checked out, you'll need to place a "hold" on the book, just as you would with a hardcover book.

Sharing Kindle books among family members

The "easy" way to share Kindle books with other family members is to register multiple Kindle devices with the same Amazon email address. For example, in my household, each Kindle device—mine, my wife's, our young daughter's—is registered to my Amazon email address. My account is used for all Kindle purchases, so each book we buy is automatically shared among all the Kindles in our household. It's convenient, but the adults in the household must take care not to purchase content that is inappropriate for youngsters.

Another way to share Kindle books is to use the Family Library function. Family Library adds more control—books may still be shared, but certain content may remain private. For example, you can link two accounts to a single device, which can enable a spouse and partner to share books. Meanwhile, those two folks can jointly supervise and control the accounts of as many as four children.

The only slight drawback with Family Library is that it takes some time to set up. For more details, visit bit.ly/FamilyLibrary .

Find Classic Freebies on Amazon and Beyond

Until now, our discussion has focused on current books—those published within the past few years and usually available free only through Amazon for a limited time. However, there is a whole new category of books freely available on Amazon and other sites.

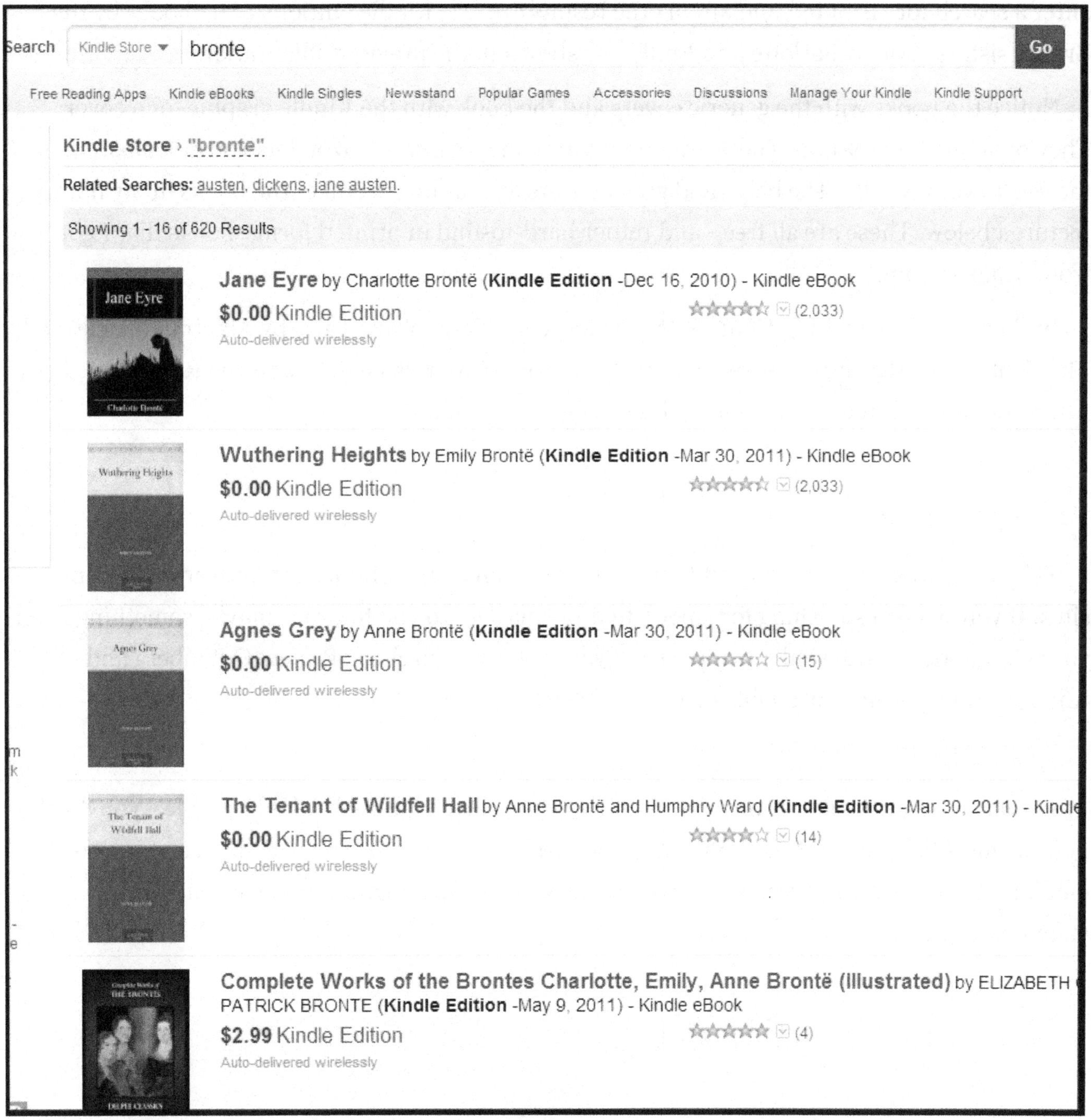

Above: Free eBooks of classic novels by the Bronte sisters.

These "Public Domain" works include the classics from authors like William Shakespreare, Jane Austen, Jules Verne, Charles Dickens, Mark Twain, and countless others. Unlike the books featured in Kindle Buffet's "Editor's Picks," these old classics remain free all year long.

These free classics can pop up any time you're browsing or searching Amazon. For example, enter a search for "Bronte," and among the results are free Kindle editions of up books by the Bronte sisters—Ann, Charlotte and Emily—as shown in the previous illustration.

Notice the books with the generic covers and the book with the Kindle graphic for a cover. They're all priced at $0.00. These are Public Domain titles, so Amazon lets you download them for free to your Kindle. The beige and green covers appear on several of the books in my library, pictured below. These are all free—and rather hard-to-find in printed form—books that I got from Amazon.com.

In the image below, King Henry V by Shakespeare, Four Weird Tales by Algernon Blackwood, The Centaur by Algernon Blackwood, The Return by Walter de la Mare and the Raven by Edgar Allen Poe were all free. Amazon has a huge collection available.

****

TIP: Many rare and out-of-print books are now available as eBooks from several different sites. If you've been searching for a book that means a lot to you to own—maybe something from your childhood or with similar sentimental value—be sure to check Project Gutenberg and Amazon. It may well be available on one of these sites.

****

Purchasing free books on Amazon. Even though a particular book might be "free," you'll still need a One-Click payment method at Amazon to download them. You'll get a receipt in your email that will show the purchase but nothing will show up on your credit card or bank statement.

Above: My Library showing several free books.

In addition to Amazon, several other websites offer vast selections of Public Domain books. The most well-known is likely Project Gutenberg, located at http://www.gutenberg.org/.

Exploring Project Gutenberg

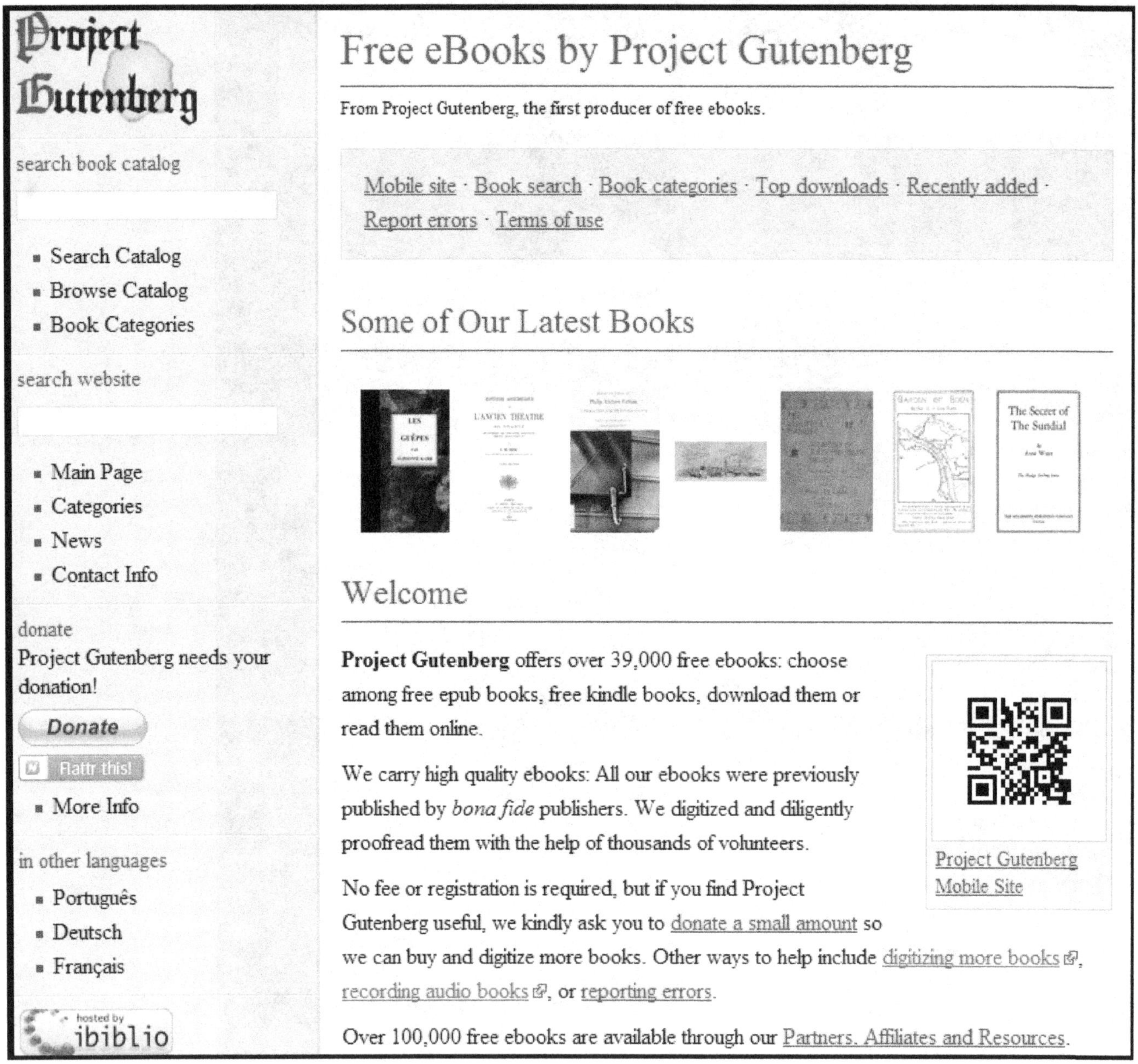

Above: The Project Gutenberg homepage

The illustration above shows the Project Gutenberg homepage. The left navigation menu gives you access to the site's entire book catalog. You can choose to **Search Catalog**, **Browse Catalog** or you can view **Book Categories**.

Let's search for a well-known suspense story, "The Turn of the Screw" by Henry James. Here is the result from Project Gutenberg:

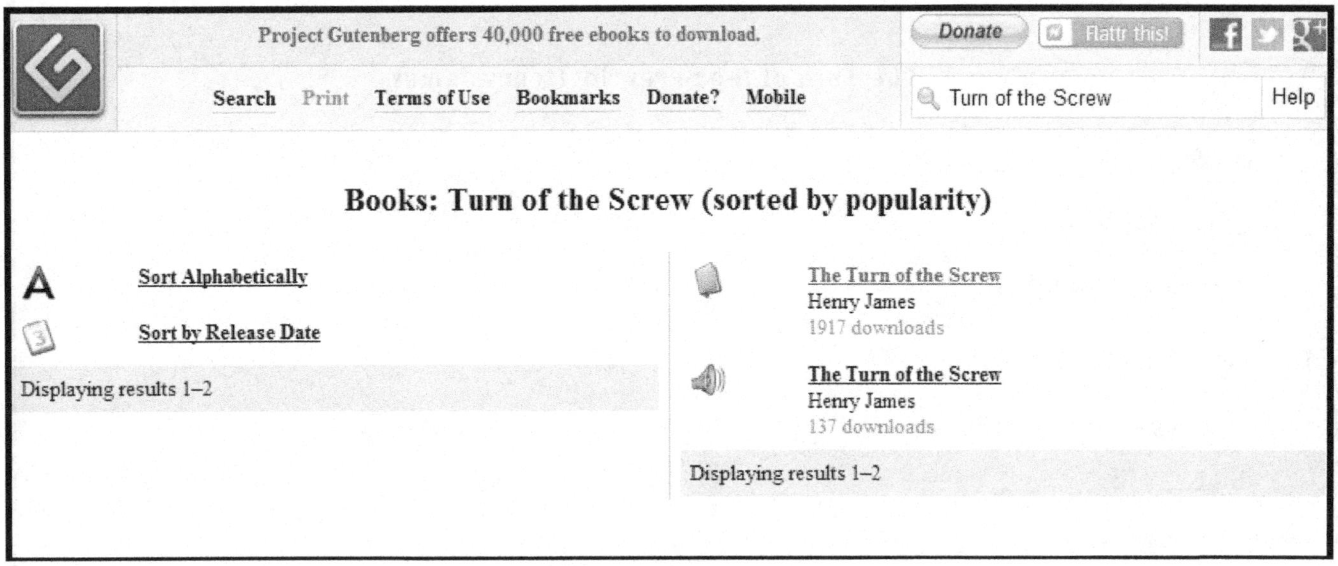

Above: Search results for 'Turn of the Screw' at Project Gutenberg.

Notice that, on the right of the page, there are two results listed. The first is a link to all the eBook versions of The Turn of the Screw. The one below it is a link to the audio version of the story. Project Gutenberg has a lot of audio books that are public domain and that are read by volunteers. If you want to stock up on audio books for a long trip, this is a good place to do it!

Let's click on the link to the eBook version of The Turn of the Screw.

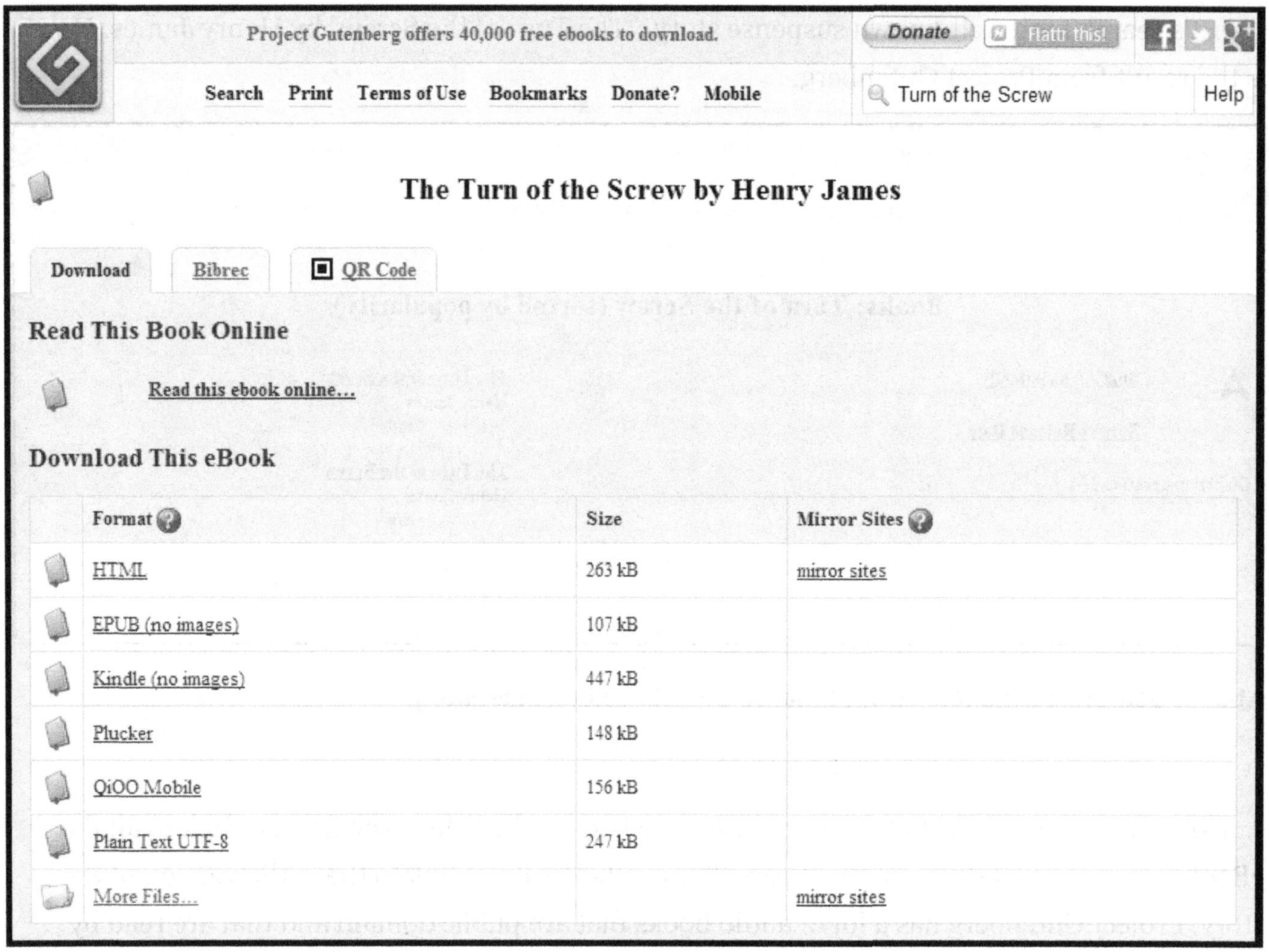

Above: The eBook Versions of 'The Turn of The Screw.'

Project Gutenberg will typically offer books in a variety of formats. Notice that there are HTML, EPUB, Kindle, PLocker, QiOO Mobile and Plain Text versions of this eBook.

Sending Personal Documents to your Kindle

You've likely got a treasure trove of reading material sitting on your computer ... or within your e-mail account. Did you know you can also enjoy this content on your Kindle?

When most people think of a "Kindle," they think of an eReader. Before the Fire came along, that's about all you could do with an eReader—read books. Back then, most eReaders came with a black-and-white display called E-ink. The older models—which are still quite popular—don't emit any light. The Kindle Fire, however, functions more like a computer monitor—generating its own light of varying colors. The reading experience is quite different, but the Fire functions quite nicely as an eReader. And although there are zillions of Kindle eBooks from which to choose, they're only the tip of the iceberg when it comes to reading on your Kindle

Using Kindle's Personal Documents Service

If you're going to use your Kindle frequently as an eReader or productivity tool, taking advantage of Amazon's Personal Documents Service is a must. Although Amazon's Kindle books use a proprietary format—you need a Kindle (or a Kindle app) to read them—you can send virtually any kind of digital document to your Kindle using the Personal Documents Service.

You can use the Personal Documents Service along with your Send-to-Kindle email address. The email address is usually formatted as follows:

[Your Name]@Kindle.com

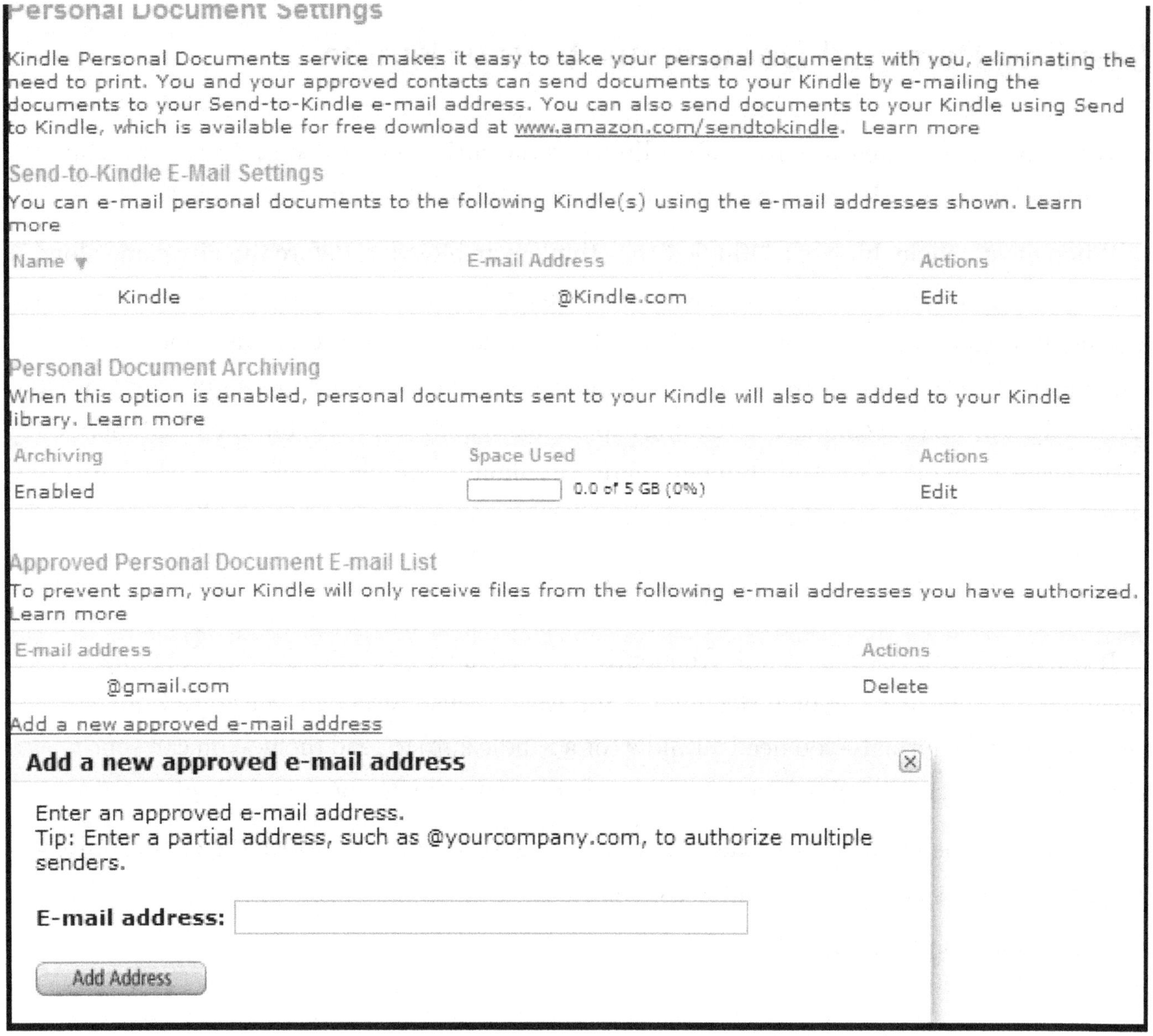

Above: Adding an email address to the Personal Document Service list at Amazon's 'Manage Your Kindle' page.

Note that the regular email address registered with your Amazon account is already added to the approved list.

Using the 'Send-to-Kindle' application on your computer

There's an alternative to the Send-to-Kindle email method that's even easier to use, especially if you forward many documents from your computer to your Kindle. Free software provided by Amazon, called the "Send-to-Kindle application," is available for PCs and Macs.

When you launch the software for the first time, you'll be asked for Amazon username and password.

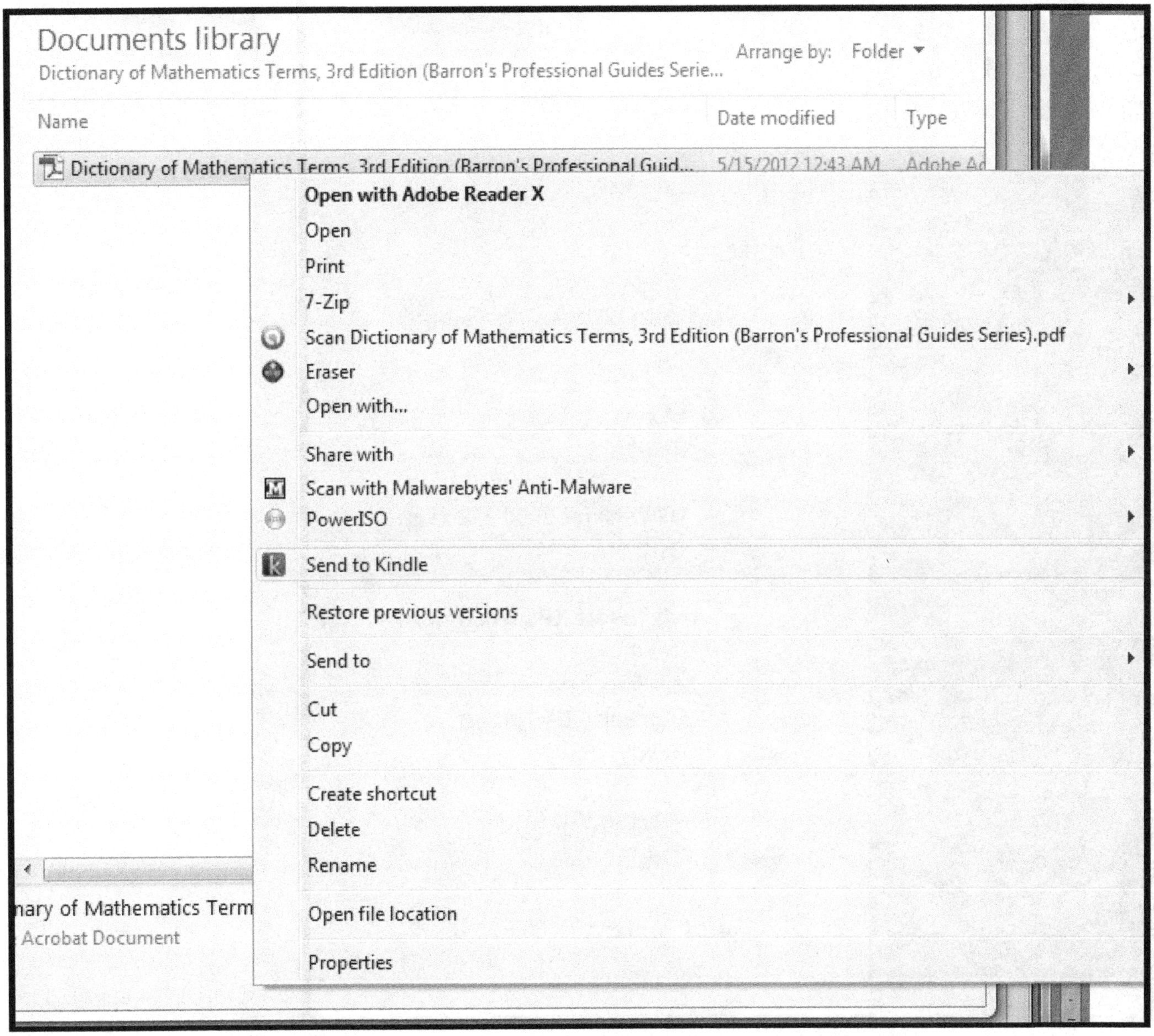

Above: Sending a document to Kindle using the Send-to-Kindle app using Windows.

The Send-to-Kindle application is quite efficient and easy to use, and it automatically converts documents to the Kindle format. After installing it on your computer, it offers two methods of sending documents. First, using your mouse, right-click on your document as illustrated below. You'll see a right-click menu with the option to "send to Kindle."

Your second option for sending documents is to use the regular "print" command while viewing your document. But instead of selecting your printer from the menu, you'll select "Send to Kindle."

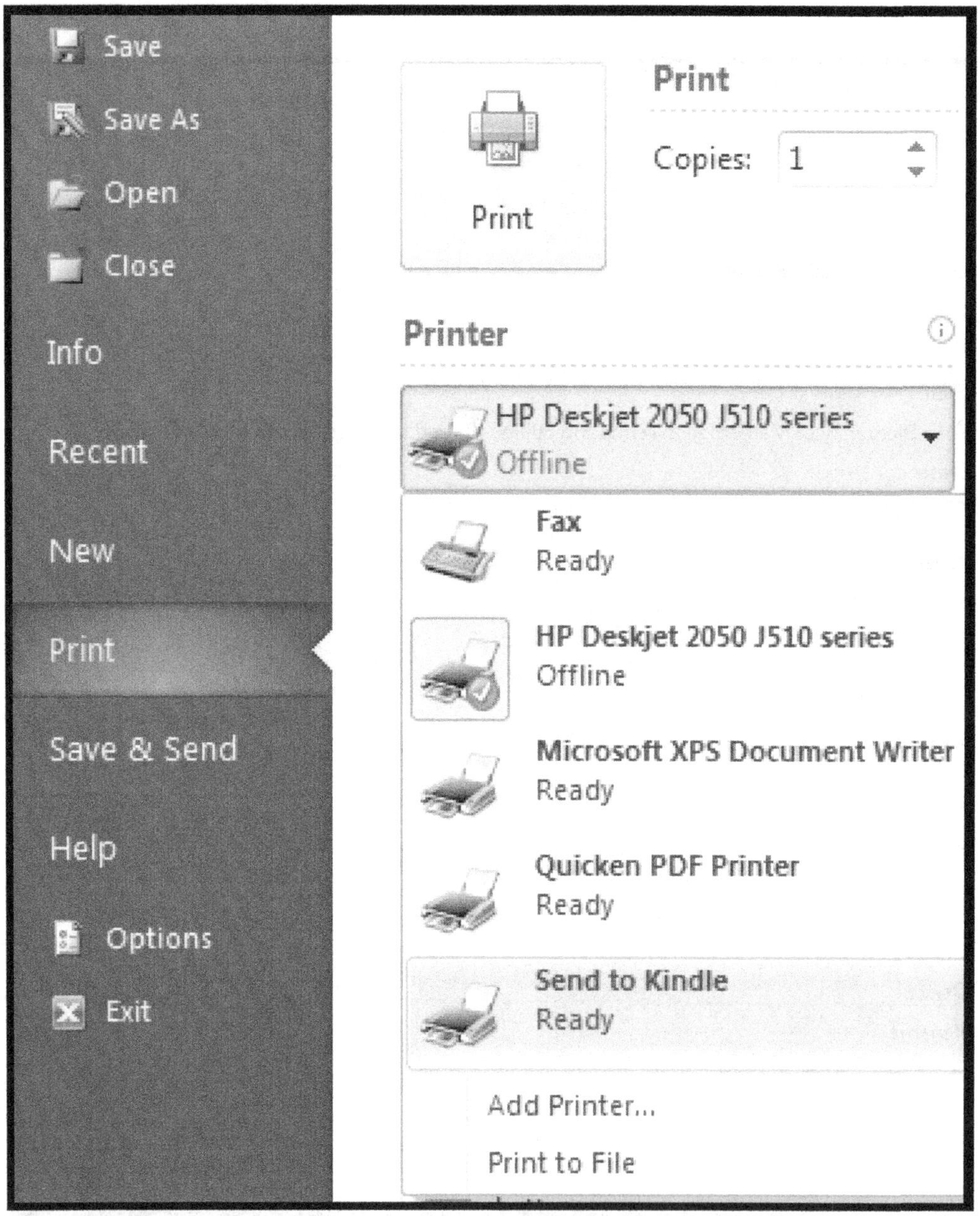

Above: The option to 'Send to Kindle' appears as a printing option after installation of the Send-to-Kindle' app.

Send to Kindle will be added as a printer option in office programs and other software that allows printing.

Using the Books 'Library'

Yet another cool feature of the Kindle is the potential for borrowing and lending Kindle eBooks. Specifically, you can:

Borrow books from your local library, when available, or;

Lend books to friends and colleagues from your Kindle.

Remember the days when you'd loan your printed books to friends, and (depending on the friend) rarely see the book again? Well, a great feature of lending books via your Kindle is that all your books will actually be returned—there's no way around it. Loans are capped at 14 days by Amazon's system.

Not all Kindle books are eligible for lending—the publisher has to agree to the program. When you're shopping for Kindle books nowadays, you'll see a notation—whether lending is "enabled" or not—in the "Product Details" of the book's listing on Amazon.

****

TIP: Remember, you can loan Kindle books to virtually anyone with an email address, regardless of whether they have a Kindle device. Kindle reading apps are available free for practically every type of computer, smartphone, and other digital gadgets.

****

Here's the procedure for lending a Kindle book:

Visit the "Manage Your Kindle" page.

Click on the "**Actions**" button on the right-hand side of the title you wish to lend. In the pop-up menu, select "Loan this title."

Next you'll arrive at this screen:

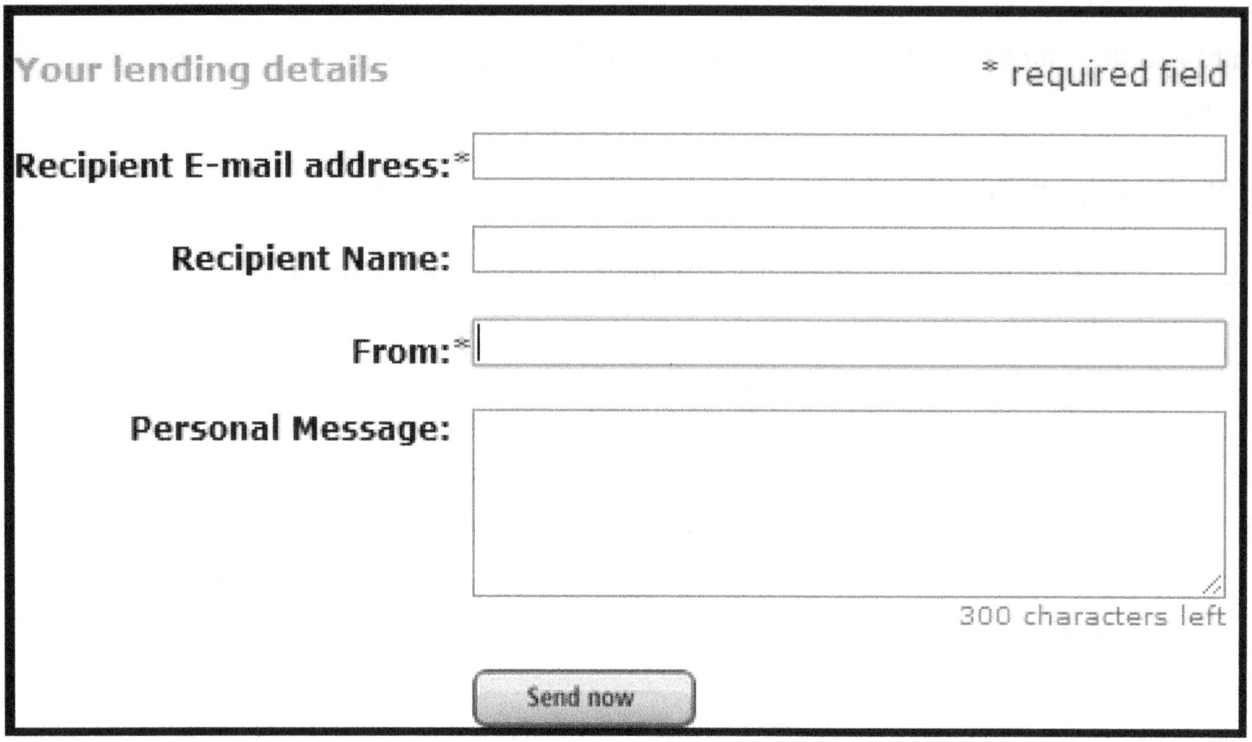

Above: Lending Details.

Simply complete the form, and your friend will receive the book. It will be returned to your library automatically in 14 days or, if the borrower finishes the book before then, it can be returned early. Remember, while your book is being borrowed, you won't have access to it on your Kindle.

Unfortunately, you may loan a Kindle book only once—that is Amazon's current policy. But I would not be surprised if the lending program, which is relatively new, is amended to be more lenient in the future.

More Free Content Using the Calibre eBook manager

Let's jump right in and download the Calibre application right now. I have been using the program, along with thousands of others, for the past three years. The best things in life are free, and believe me, Calibre is one of them.

Go to http://calibre-ebook.com/ and select "Download Calibre"

Open the downloaded program to install the package once it's completed

On your first run, you'll get the **Welcome Wizard**. This is designed to help you set up your libraries and to import your books, as well as to help you select the correct device!

The first screen, pictured below, will set your **Calibre Library** directory. The default choice is a good one.

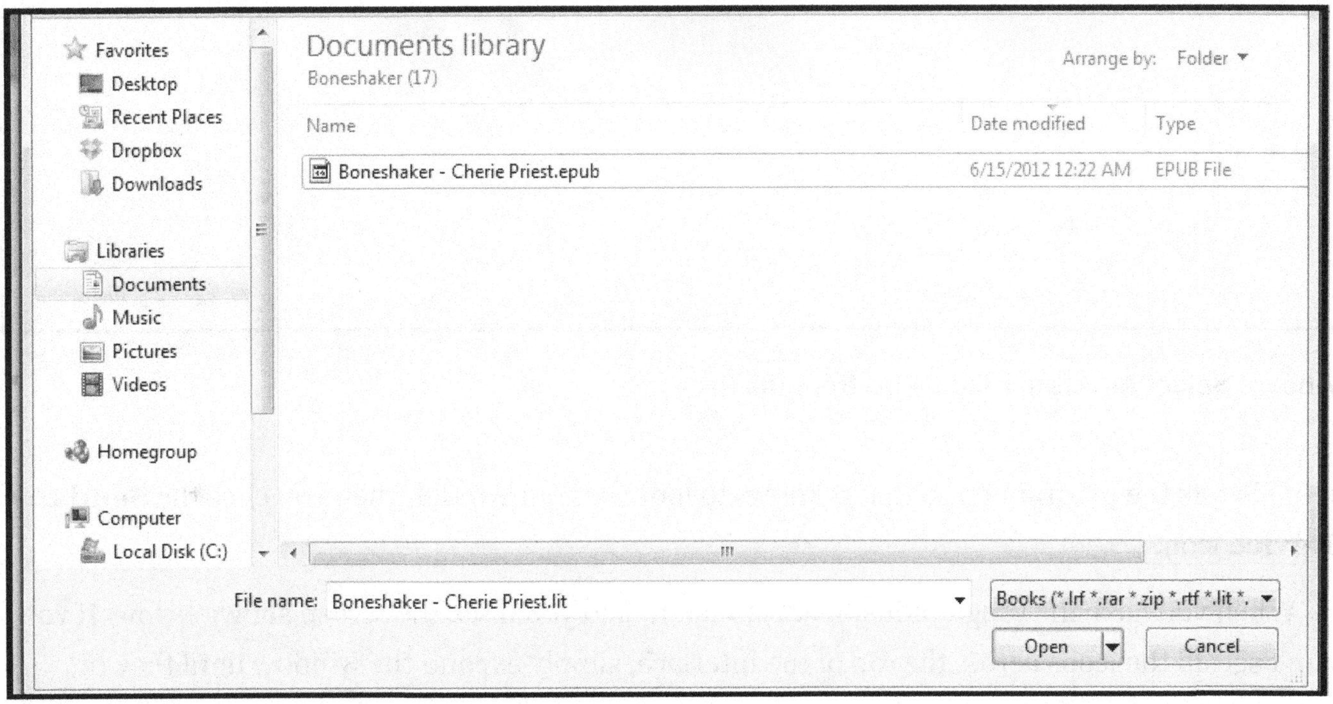

Above: The Calibre Welcome Wizard screen 1

On the next screen, you'll have to choose your device. Obviously, choose Kindle Fire!

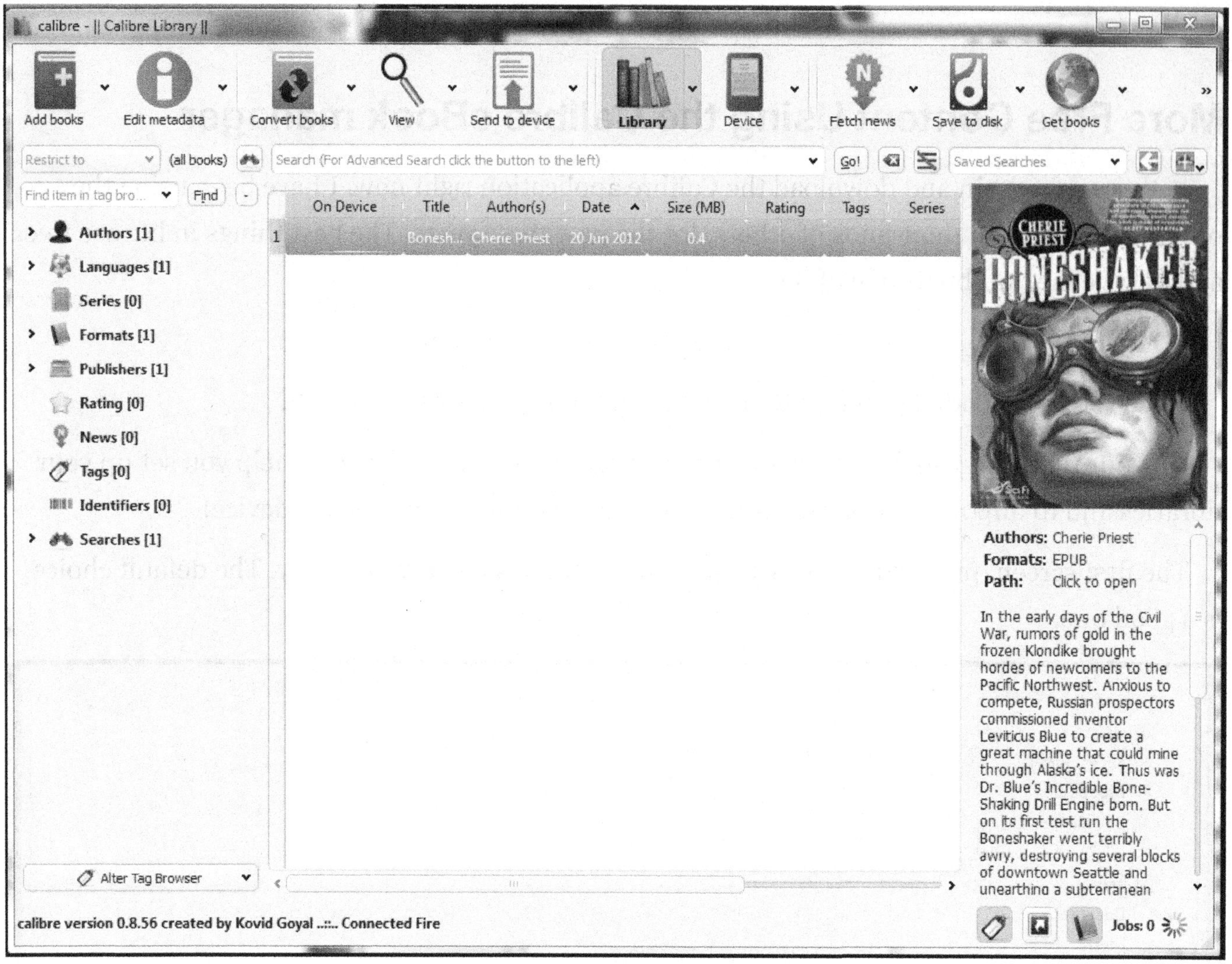

Above: Select Amazon, Kindle Fire from the list.

This sets the program up so that it knows to look for your Kindle when you click the **Send to Device** icon.

When you have the program installed, launch it, and you'll see the screen shown below. If you can't see all the icons across the top of the interface, simply expand the window until they fit.

Study the interface for a moment. This program is capable of doing many things; even offering you a way to shop for content across a number of different stores. What we'll concern ourselves with first, however, is opening up new sources of literature by using the features built into this program that allow you to convert books from other formats into ones that your Amazon Kindle can read.

All the news you can eat, and Calibre picks up the check

OK, I'll admit it. I'm a book nut. But I have an even bigger problem. I'm addicted to newspapers, too. I was a "news junkie" before anyone ever heard of such a thing. Twenty-five years ago, I paid about $75 a month to have three different newspapers dropped at my doorstep every morning—my local paper, The Wall Street Journal, and the New York Times. Now, since I discovered Calibre, I've been reading six newspapers a day—plus bunch of blogs and magazines like Newsweek and Time—and it doesn't cost me one red cent. The New York Times. The Washington Post. The New York Post. And, if I still have time, I can read The Onion and a couple others—just to get my humor fix. Your local newspaper is probably available, too. Calibre downloads the content they post on their websites, and sends it, nicely formatted, to your Kindle. The only cost is the few minutes you'll spend setting it up once, and then it works every day. Here how to get started:

Click on "**Fetch News**" in the Menu.

Select your language.

Select a news source.

In the illustration below, you can see that I've selected The Washington Post.

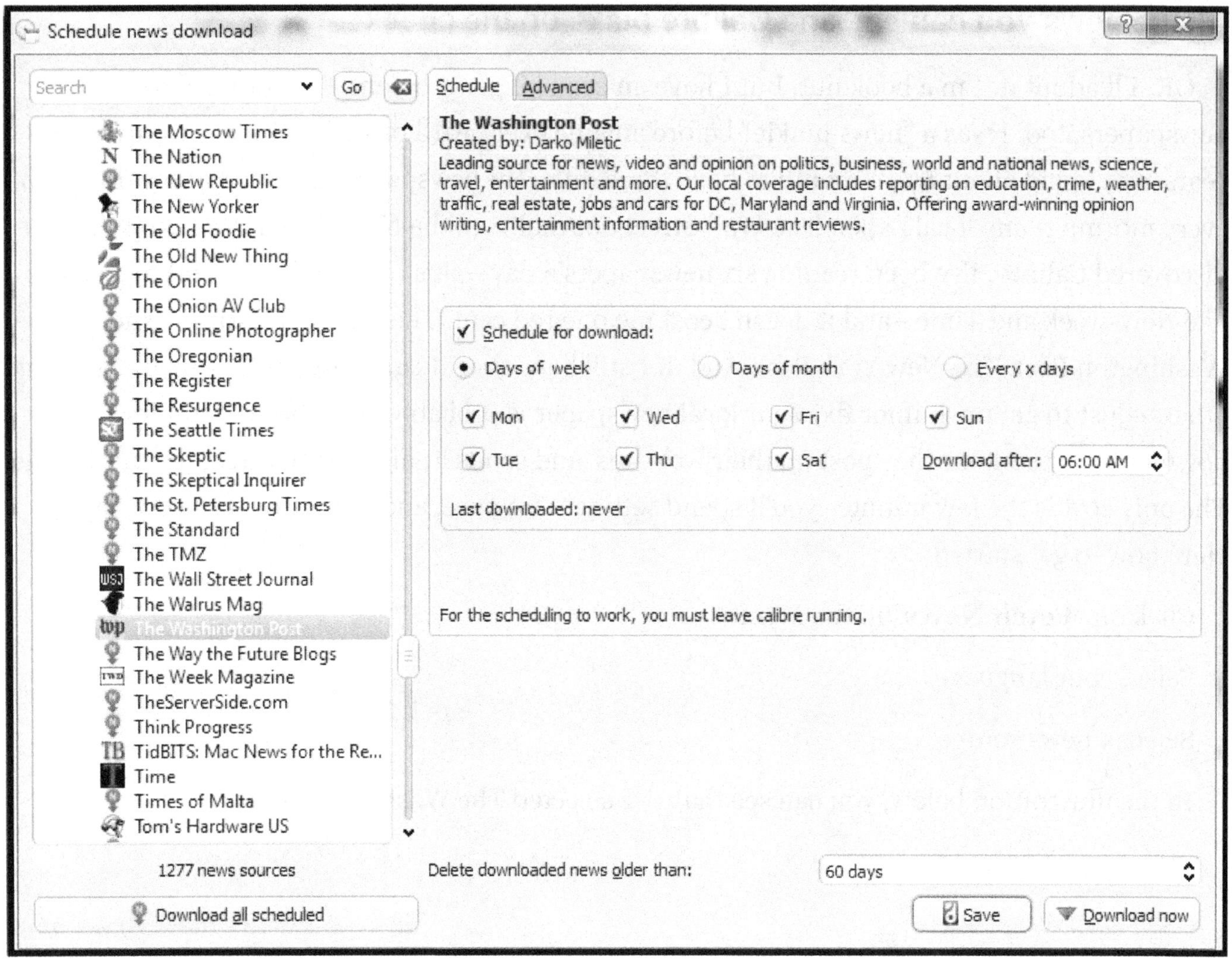

Above: Selecting the Washington Post.

Note that I've opted to have it download automatically every day of the week after 6am. If you were the ultimate news junkie, you could set it to download the Associated Press news wire every 10 minutes. Calibre has hundreds of different news sources available in a huge number of languages, you just click them and enjoy—free.

Of course, you have to leave Calibre running so it automatically downloads your news sources. If you have several news sites on your list, it will take a while. Personally, I leave my computer on 24/7, and Calibre is finding news for me constantly, and feeding my Kindle. In the old days, I used to finish my three newspapers and still want more. Now, with Calibre, I don't have a prayer of skimming everything I'm tempted to read every day.

****

TIP: In this section, we're talking about downloading content for free. It sounds too good to be true, but it's totally above board. We're not stealing, we're just using the stuff that publishers are posting to their websites. Calibre simply does the work of formatting it for the Kindle and email it to us.

****

After the news site has converted, you'll be able to transfer it to your Kindle using the same interface that you use to transfer books. One of the best things about the Calibre program is that it's smart in meaningful ways. The program, for instance, will transfer newspapers to your Newsstand.

Above: The Newsstand after transferring the converted news site.

Opening up the converted newspaper will give you a listing of all the articles it contains, separated by sections.

Above: The converted newspaper's Table of Contents.

Tap any article to open it up and you'll be presented with the full text of the articles, and perhaps the photos, depending on the publication. Even better, the article opens up in the same comfortable format as the **Reading View** option in your browser for websites, which you can see in the illustration below.

So, is there any real difference between reading a newspaper website in reading view in your browser and reading it converted from Calibre? The main difference is that the newspaper's table of contents is presented in a way that is much more workable with a touch-screen device. The same applies to magazines that are converted in this way.

WORLD · AFGHAN REFUGEES FORCED TO RETURN HOME

Afghan refugees forced to return home

By Kevin Sieff,

Kabul — During the last stretch of his family's journey home, Esmatullah perched atop a truckload of kitchenware, firewood and furniture, hurtling toward Kabul while the evidence of three decades in exile shifted beneath him.

On either side of the truck, the bazaars grew denser. The buildings became taller and more fortified. American convoys snaked through traffic, heading downtown.

Nearly two days after leaving their home in Pakistan, Esmatullah and his 22 relatives had made it to Afghanistan's capital, after 30 years as refugees. They looked out at their country. They tried not to panic.

The uncertainty shrouding Afghanistan's future has prompted thousands of Afghans to seek an escape route — foreign visa applications, asylum pleas, long journeys across the border. But every day, families swim against that current, returning to Afghanistan after years

Above: The article presentation in a converted newspaper.

eBooks, Calibre, and the Kindle

Believe it or not, there's more to the story. You can manage eBooks—downloaded from Amazon and elsewhere—using Calibre.

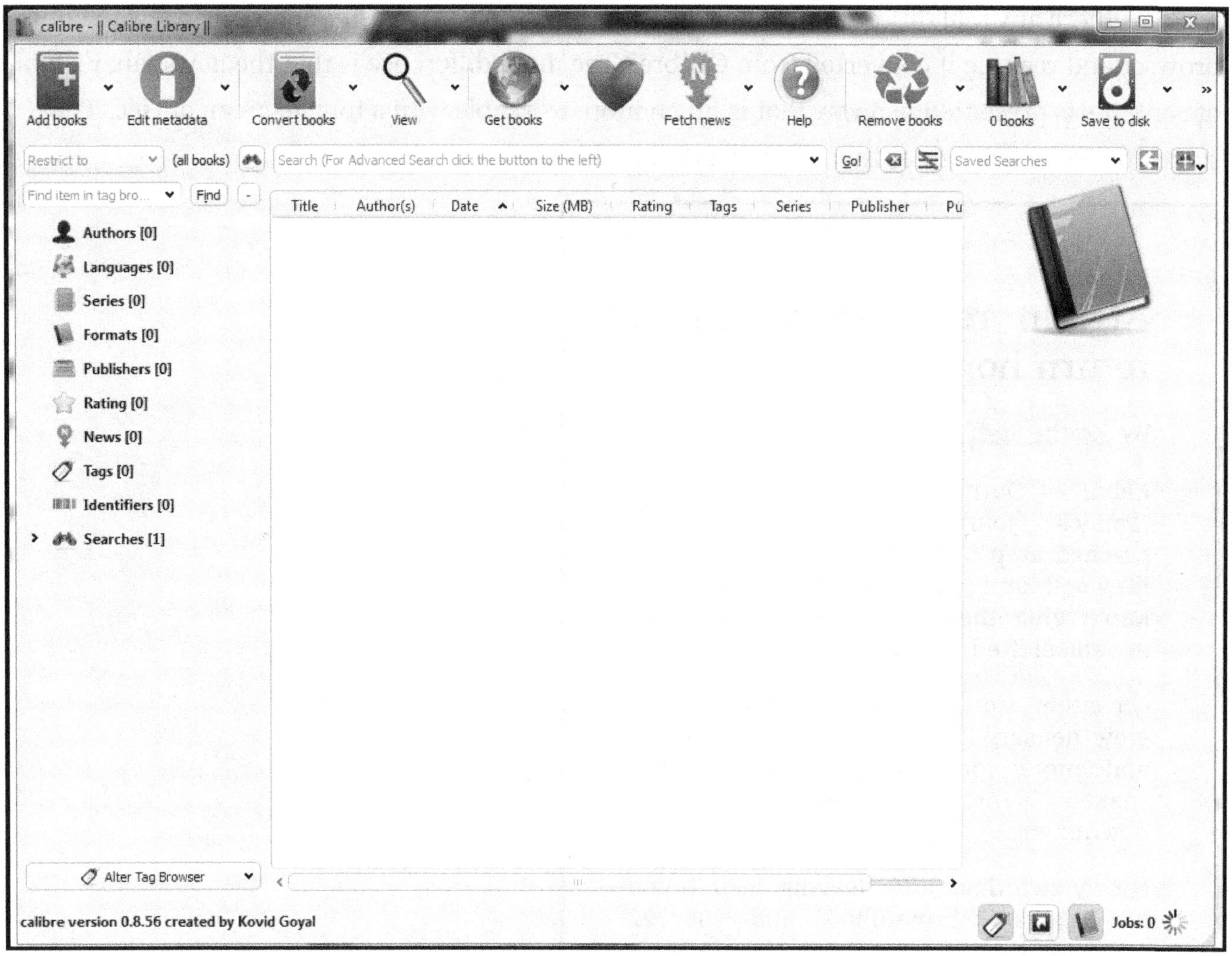

Above: Calibre's main screen

In the illustration, I haven't added my eBooks to the collection yet, so the middle of the screen is blank. There are many ways you can add books to your library. By default, they're sent to the **Calibre Library** folder.

The **Add Books** icon appears at the upper left. Select it, and you'll see the options shown below.

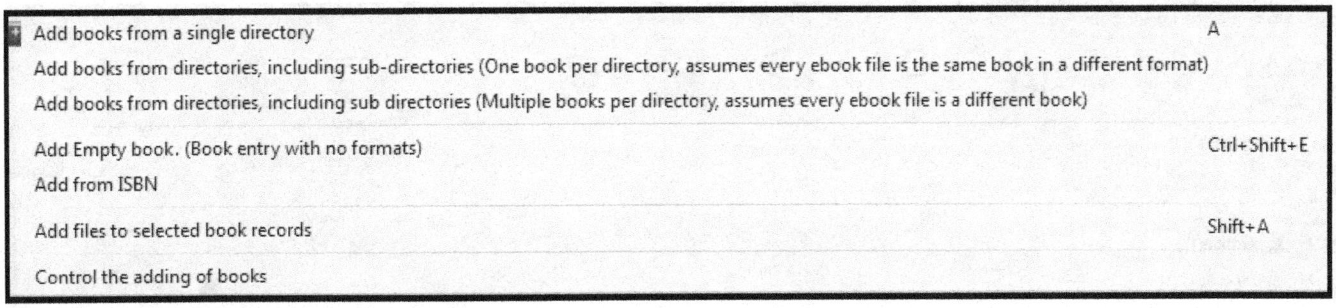

Above: The Add Books dialog

There are quite a few options here, but we'll concentrate adding one book to the library in a format that Kindle just doesn't like.

In this case, I'm going to add a book that's stored in the EPUB format—a popular one on many sites—but that I want to read on my Amazon Kindle in the native Kindle AZW or MOBI format.

To start, click on "**Add books from a single directory**" and browse to the directory that you want. In the illustration below, I've chosen the book "pg1062.epub" which is actually The Raven by Edgar Allen Poe, which I have in the EPUB format that the Kindle will not read. I downloaded it from Project Gutenberg, a site that has plenty of public domain eBooks to choose from.

In the illustration above, you can see that the book has been added to my **Calibre Library**. Notice that even the cover art came over with the import, as did the description and other metatag information. This is one of the handiest features with the Calibre program. I'll change it to more suitable cover art and change the metatags during the conversion process so that they're more descriptive and accurate.

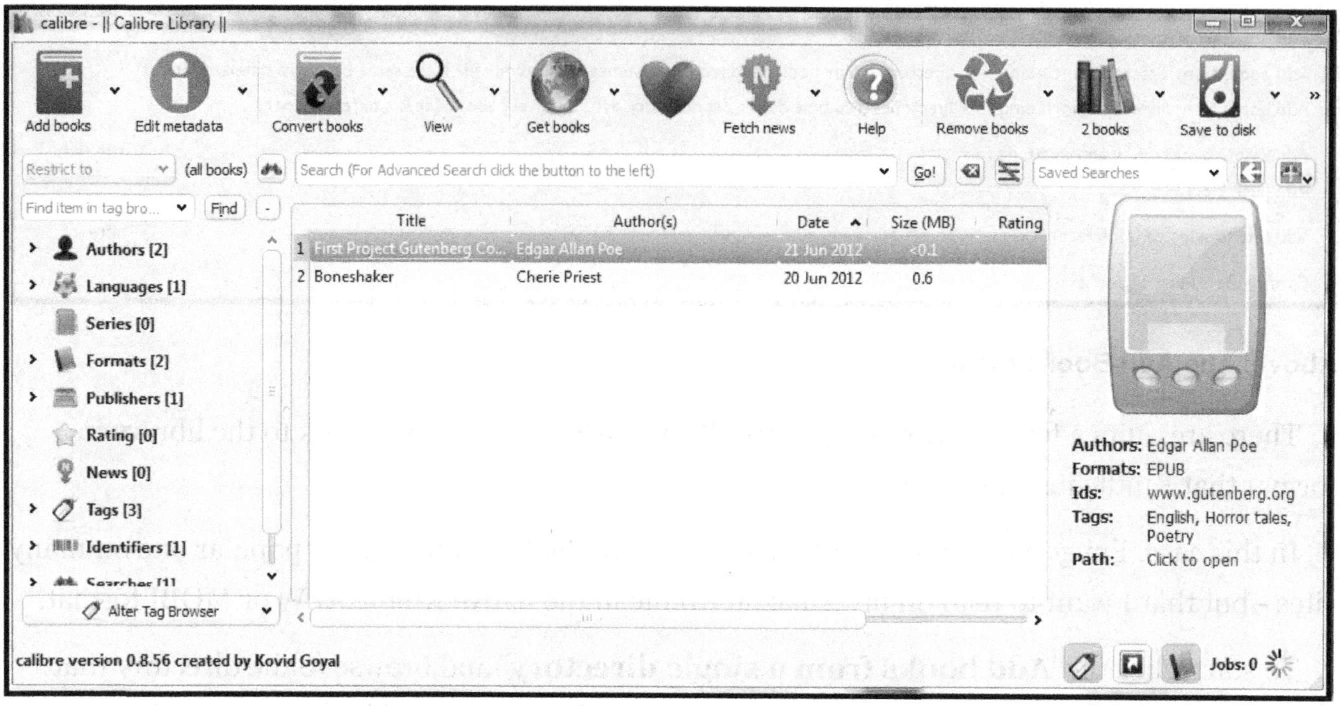

Above: The EBook from Project Gutenberg now appears in My Library.

Before I dump this to my Kindle, I have to convert it. Fortunately, Calibre makes that very easy to do.

Highlight the title and select the "**Convert Books**" icon and then select "**Convert individually**", as shown below.

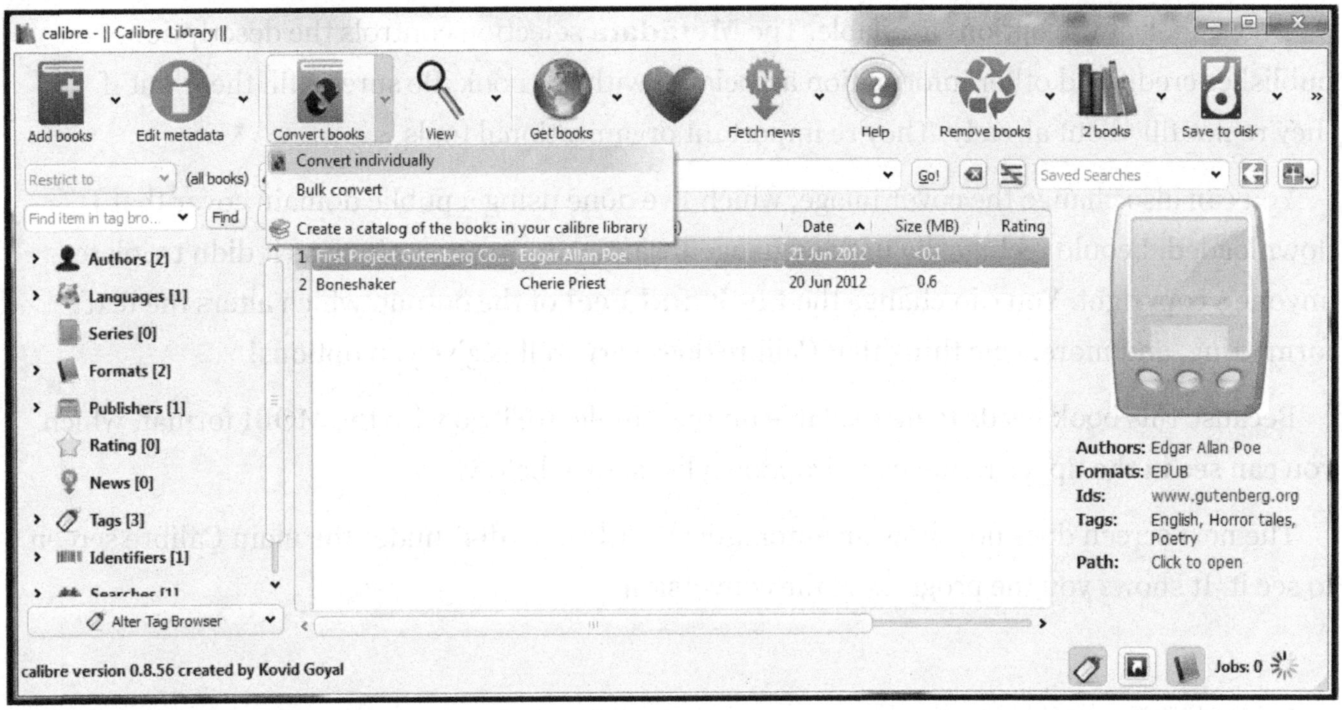

Above: Getting Ready to Covert

Once you select "**Convert individually**", the screen pictured next will appear.

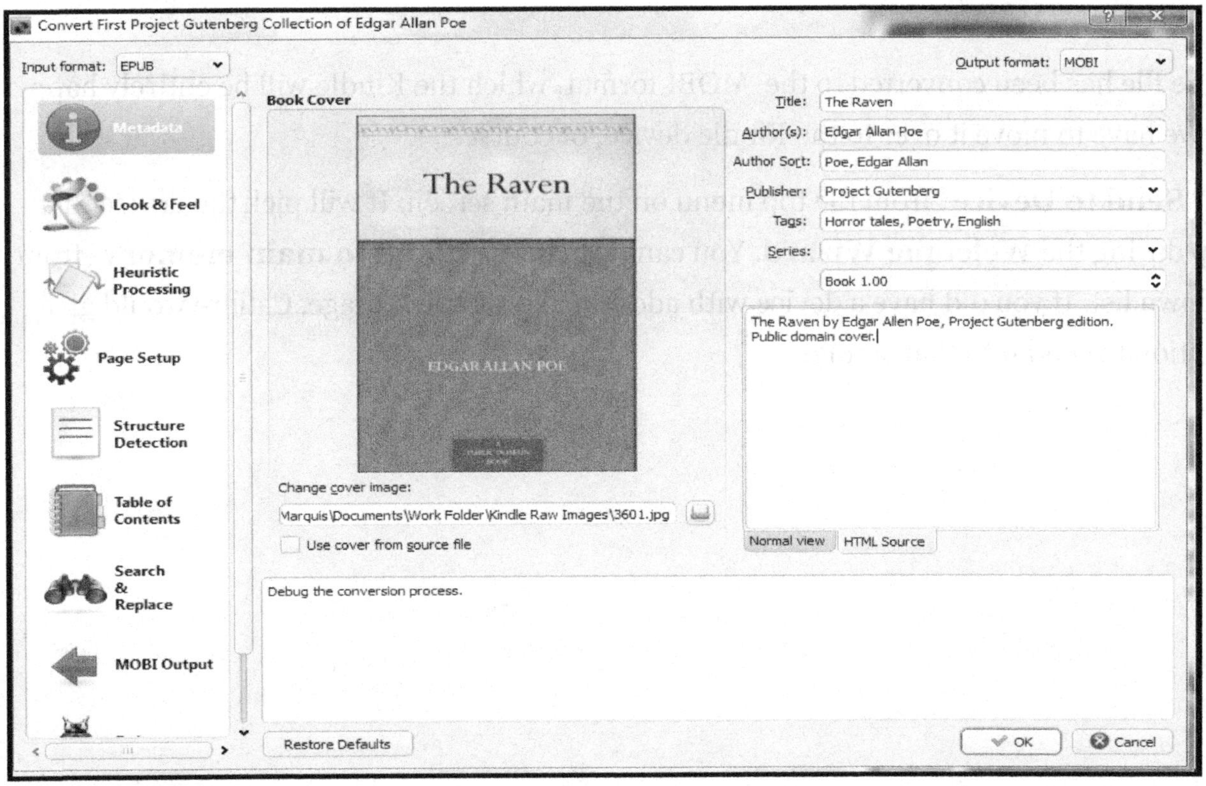

Above: The Convert screen

Take a look at the options available. The **Metadata** selection controls the description, publisher credit and other information associated with the book. Be sure to fill these out if they're not filled out already. They're important organizational tools.

You can also change the cover image, which I've done using a public domain cover that I downloaded. I could technically use any image I wanted, however, as long as it didn't violate anyone's copyright. You can change the **Look and Feel** of the output, which alters the text formatting, and more. One thing that Calibre does very well is give you options!

Because this book needs to be readable on the Kindle, we'll go with the MOBI format, which you can see in the upper right-most dropdown list shown below.

The next screen does not show up automatically. Click "**Jobs**" under the main Calibre screen to see it. It shows you the progress of the conversion.

****

TIP: You can convert more than one file at once, but it takes a lot of time. If you're going to do so, you might want to get a cup of coffee, order a pizza or do something else to pass the time. If you have a slow computer, consider making your own pizza from scratch!

****

Now, the file has been converted to the MOBI format, which the Kindle will be entirely happy with, but we have to move it over to the Kindle device, of course.

Select, "**Send to Device**" from the top menu on the main screen. It will pick the device that you set up during the **Welcome Wizard**. You can just choose "**Send to main memory**" from the dropdown list. If you did have a device with additional onboard storage, Calibre would give you the option to send it to that storage.

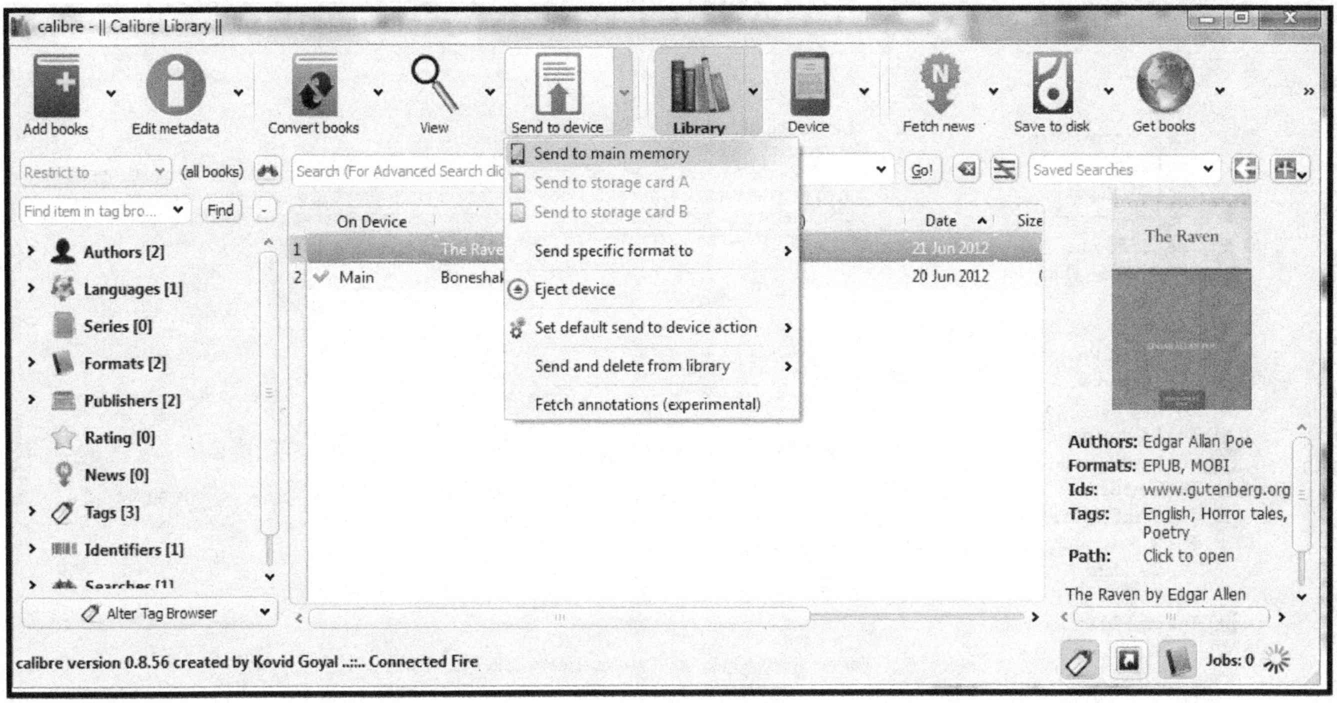

Above: Sending the book to the Kindle.

When the book has been sent, you'll see the listing for it under the "On Device" heading change, as shown below.

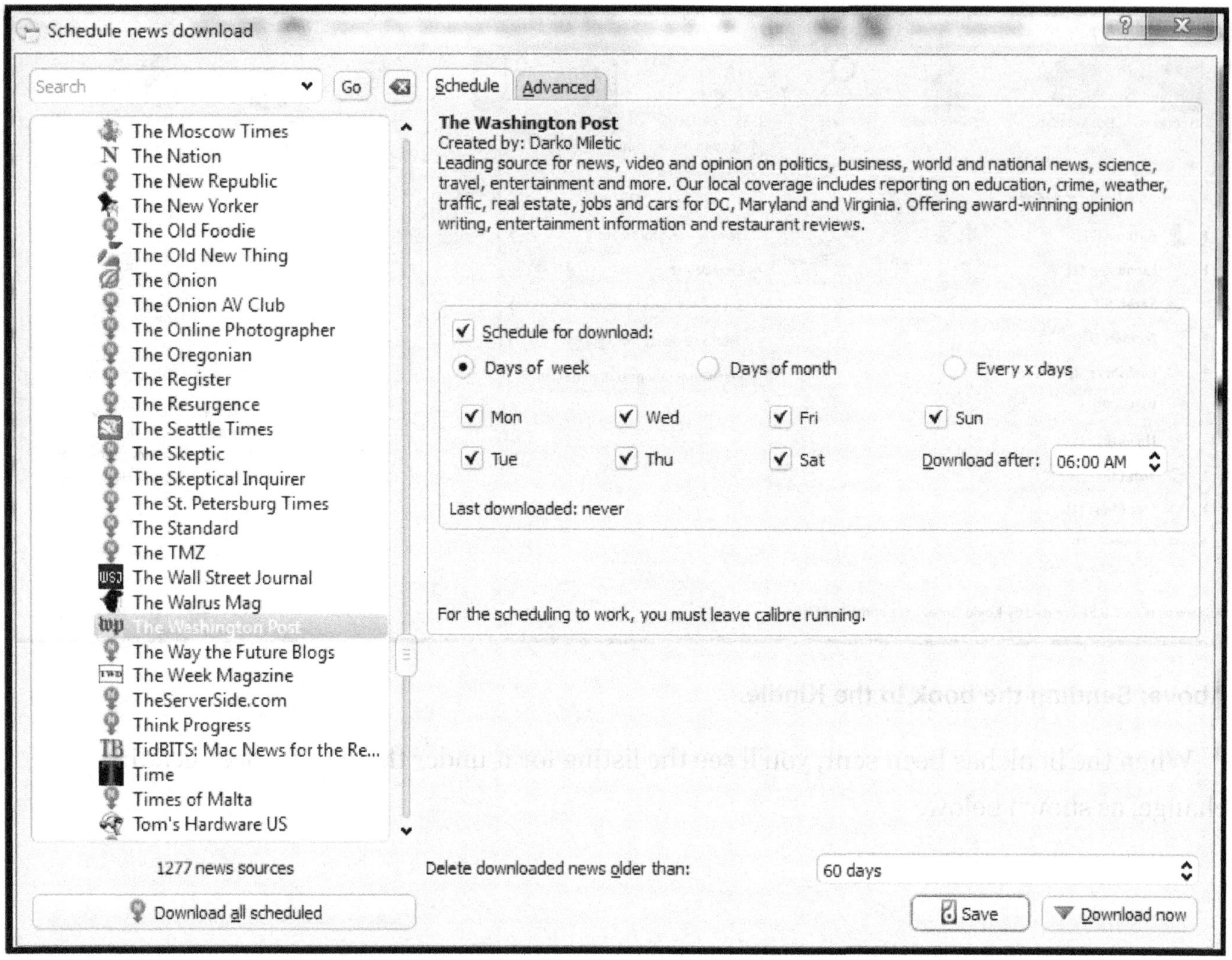

Above: The book now appears on my device.

If I go to my **Books** library on my Kindle Fire and look under the titles available on my device, it shows right up, as pictured below.

Above: The Raven, Converted to a New Format.

This is only one of the functions that Calibre offers you. It's an amazingly powerful program. We'll explore it more, but be aware that this is going to be one of your most important resources for getting free books off of the Internet. The sites that offer public domain works sometimes don't have them in a format that the Kindle reads. In the future, of course, a format may come along that is incompatible with your Kindle books. Instead of having to buy them in a new format, you'll just be able to convert them!

****

Briefly: For the love of Calibre

Calibre is the invention of a developer named Kovid Goyal. Though he started the program, it now has many different contributors that keep adding to it, improving it and developing it in new and creative ways. It's a labor of love, and the program is released under the GPL license, which means that it's free for everyone to use as much as they want.

Donations are accepted for this program, so I encourage you to contribute if you benefit from it as I have. Visit http://calibre-ebook.com.

****

Exploring Calibre Further

Calibre has numerous other features. The ways you can use it to enhance your experience using your Kindle Fire are many and, doubtless, you'll find your own ways of using it to make your experience with eBooks, new sources and other media much more enjoyable.

You'll find plenty of documentation and technical information for this program located at http://manual.calibre-ebook.com/. The online manual will let you explore the other functions of this program.

If you don't feel like wading through the online technical documentation, there is an intro video that gives you a nice overview of some of the features discussed in this chapter and more located on the Calibre homepage.

Kindlefeeder

Another popular third-party Kindle service is Kindlefeeder. Like Calibre, it enables you to send content that appears on the Internet to your Kindle via email. I suppose it's a bit more easy-to-use at first, but doesn't have the range of Calibre.

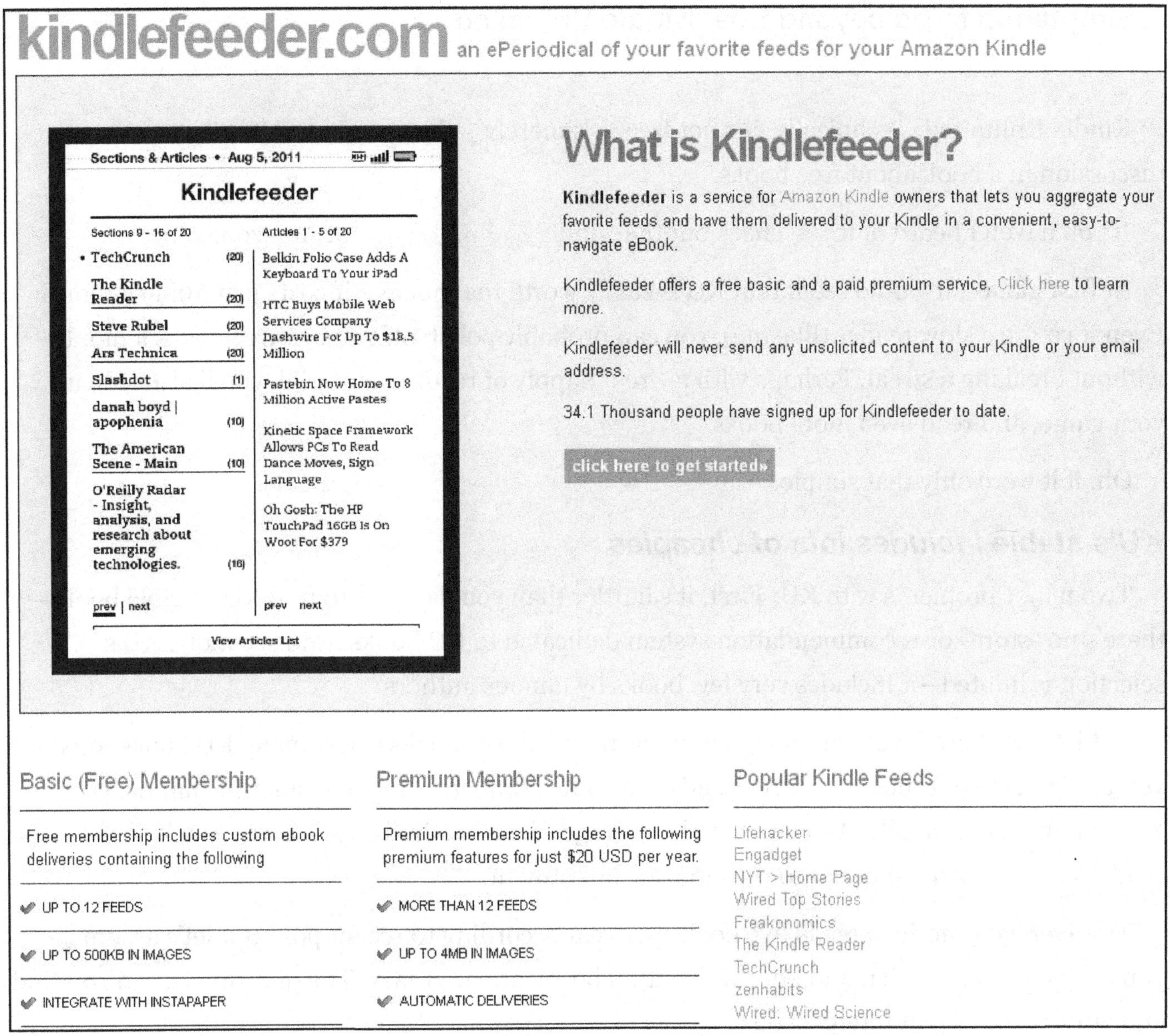
kindlefeeder.com an ePeriodical of your favorite feeds for your Amazon Kindle
Sections & Articles • Aug 5, 2011
Kindlefeeder
Sections 9 - 16 of 20
Articles 1 - 5 of 20
TechCrunch (20)
The Kindle Reader (20)
Steve Rubel (20)
Ars Technica (20)
Slashdot (1)
danah boyd | apophenia (10)
The American Scene - Main (10)
O'Reilly Radar - Insight, analysis, and research about emerging technologies. (16)
Belkin Folio Case Adds A Keyboard To Your iPad
HTC Buys Mobile Web Services Company Dashwire For Up To $18.5 Million
Pastebin Now Home To 8 Million Active Pastes
Kinetic Space Framework Allows PCs To Read Dance Moves, Sign Language
Oh Gosh: The HP TouchPad 16GB Is On Woot For $379
prev | next
prev next
View Articles List
What is Kindlefeeder?
Kindlefeeder is a service for Amazon Kindle owners that lets you aggregate your favorite feeds and have them delivered to your Kindle in a convenient, easy-to-navigate eBook.
Kindlefeeder offers a free basic and a paid premium service. Click here to learn more.
Kindlefeeder will never send any unsolicited content to your Kindle or your email address.
34.1 Thousand people have signed up for Kindlefeeder to date.
click here to get started»
Basic (Free) Membership
Free membership includes custom ebook deliveries containing the following
UP TO 12 FEEDS
UP TO 500KB IN IMAGES
INTEGRATE WITH INSTAPAPER
Premium Membership
Premium membership includes the following premium features for just $20 USD per year.
MORE THAN 12 FEEDS
UP TO 4MB IN IMAGES
AUTOMATIC DELIVERIES
Popular Kindle Feeds
Lifehacker
Engadget
NYT > Home Page
Wired Top Stories
Freakonomics
The Kindle Reader
TechCrunch
zenhabits
Wired: Wired Science

A temptation to go beyond free: Kindle Unlimited

Kindle Unlimited. Technically, it's not free. It's merely "all you can eat." But it merits some discussion in a book about free books.

If you haven't heard of it yet, check out the Kindle Unlimited hub at Amazon.com:

At first glance, it would seem that KU is easily worth the money—it costs just $9.99 a month. Even if you're a slow reader (like me), you can probably polish off two or three books a month without breaking a sweat. Perhaps with a "free" supply of reading material, you'll also step up your game, and read even more books.

Oh, if it were only that simple.

KU's stable includes lots of cheapies

Two major problems with KU: First, it's harder than you'd expect to find KU-eligible books—there's no "store" or recommendation system dedicated to KU books. And secondly, KU's selection is limited—it includes very few books by famous authors.

But let's say you're patient enough to unearth lots of KU books—how many KU books must you read to get your money's worth? Let's run some numbers. First, consider the annual cost of KU, about $120 annually. And let's say the average cost of a Kindle book is $6. You'll need to read 20 books during the year to recoup your investment.

The average American reads five books per year according to recent poll. But let's assume you're a voracious reader, and knocking out 20 books a year is easy. The question is, can you find enough KU books that interest you?

Here's a quick experiment: Run through the list of books you've purchased over the past year. To see a list of your Amazon Kindle purchases, visit www.bit.ly/KindleOrders . Here are the books you've spent your hard-earned dollars on.

Now, determine how many of those books you bought are KU-eligible. Probably not too many. Personally, I bought 27 Kindle books during 2014, and just four of those are available through Kindle Unlimited.

Here's another way to evaluate KU's value. Instead of looking at your previous purchases, consider your Amazon wishlist (if you have one) or your Goodreads "want to read" list. How many of those books are in KU? Not many, right?

Why the dearth of selection in KU? Quite simply, leading authors aren't in the program because it doesn't pay them enough. Danielle Steel? No. Nora Roberts? Nope. Robert Ludlum? Nada. James Patterson, John Grisham, Dan Brown, Ken Follett, Stephenie Meyer, Mary Higgins Clark, Patricia Cornwell, Tom Clancy, Janet Evanovich or Dr. Seuss? Sorry, Charlie.

Oh, and this leads to another complication. Most of the no-name books included in KU are already priced low—$2.99 and under. So you'll have to read at least 40 books a year to make KU pay off, not the 20 books we assumed earlier.

Now certainly, one thing we've overlooked in this exercise: the availability of KU would likely increase your consumption of books. You just might discover five or more "favorite" authors over the course of the next year during your use of KU. You might feel the freedom to sample a genre that you've never explored before. One or more of these new books might, quite literally, change your life. That, after all, is the power of reading.

Above: Here's a portion of Amazon's product page for a book. If the book is KU-eligible, it will have the two features circled above: the KU logo at the left, and the "Read for Free" button at the right.

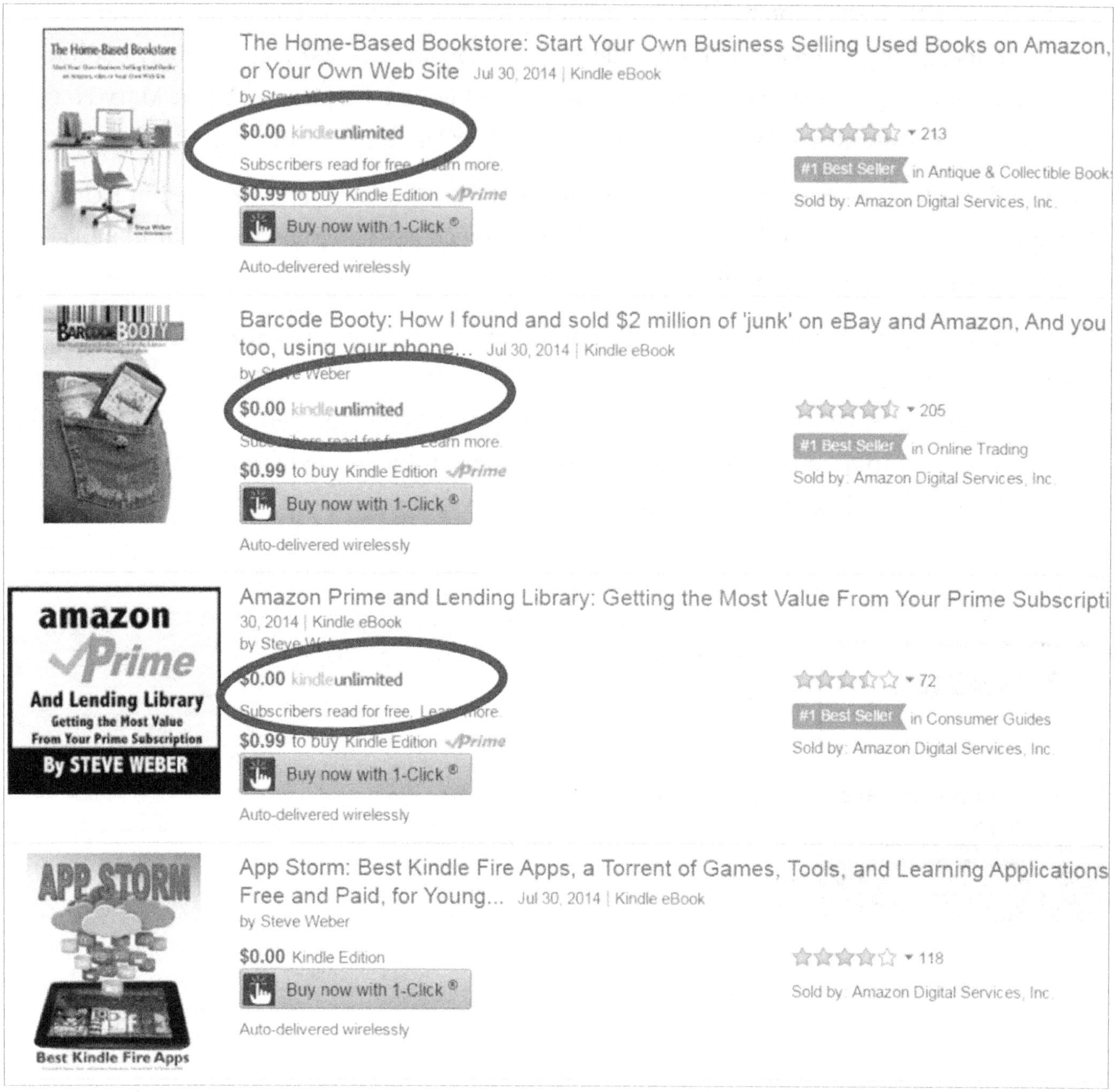

Above: Here's another way to identify KU-eligible books. The image above shows Amazon's search results for the author name "Steve Weber." KU books are identified by the logo under the author name.

The dearth of selection in KU

Why doesn't KU include the popular books most people want to read? It's simple: KU pays authors and publishers a pittance compared to what they're used to. KU pays about $1.35 per book to authors instead of the $2 to $8 per book these folks are used to. As a result, the "big five" publishing houses—HarperCollins, Hachette, Macmillan, Penguin Random House and Simon &

Shuster—aren't in KU. The KU catalog includes about 1 million titles, compared to the 3.5 million Kindle books available otherwise.

Now, you might be muttering to yourself, "KU would be doing just fine if it weren't for those greedy authors and publishers." Perhaps. But this won't change overnight. As a result, KU is saddled with lots of books from relatively unknown authors who often don't have the resources to pay for professional editors, proofreaders, and audiobook narrators.

KU is more appealing at first

During your first month, the free trial, you might be looking at KU through rose-colored glasses. The program seems awesome in the beginning, partly because of some special deals Amazon has arranged with a few famous authors. Amazon bought the rights to add Harry Potter, Lord of the Rings, and Hunger Games to KU, and these books are displayed prominently. After that, the hits are few and far between. Not a single major publisher in the United States has signed onto KU. (If Amazon were able to attract one or two of the biggies, the value of KU would increase considerably.)

KU books are hard to find

Not only are there few books available through KU, Amazon hasn't made KU-eligible books easy to find. There's a KU logo that appears on the book's webpage, but the logo doesn't appear on most category pages or bestseller rankings—making KU books sometimes as hard to find as a needle in a haystack.

One of the greatest things about Amazon is its book recommendation system. The website suggests books based on your previous purchases and ratings—visit the address: bit.ly/KindleRecommendations. But which one of these books are available through KU? There's no way to know unless you click through to each one, a tedious process.

You can also browse part of the KU catalog by using a Kindle device. Click on the shopping-cart logo, then look under the **Featured** heading for **Kindle Unlimited**. You'll see a list of books, which you can sort by popularity, genre, customer rating, or release date. For KU-eligible books, you'll find the Kindle Unlimited logo alongside the book: kindleunlimited. Unfortunately, if you search for a specific title or author, your search results will include non-KU books.

Alternatives to KU

Although Amazon's Kindle system undoubtedly has the broadest selection of eBooks, some competing subscription programs offer more of the books from major publishers.

Entitle (www.entitlebooks.com) has the best selection of bestsellers, including new releases from HarperCollins and Simon & Shuster. You can access up to two books at a time for $9.99 a month, three books at a time for $14.99 per month, or 24 for $99 a year. Also, Entitle works with Barnes & Noble Nook eReaders, while other services mentioned here require an Android or Apple device.

Oyster (www.oysterbooks.com) has a fantastic selection of older books, but not many current bestsellers. The company charges $9.95 a month for unlimited access to its catalog using an app. Oyster claims about 500,000 titles. No titles from major publishers.

Scribd (www.scribd.com) provides access to 400,000 documents for $8.99 a month. No titles from major publishers.

Made in the USA
Monee, IL
08 November 2026

67380766R00031